M000082069

LiFe

THE FINAL FRONTIER

LIFE

THE FINAL FRONTIER

TIM JOYCE

AND

CARL KOZLOWSKI

Andrews McMeel
Publishing

Kansas City

Life: The Final Frontier copyright © 2001 by Tim Joyce and Carl Kozlowski. All rights reserved. Printed in the United States of America. No part of this book may be used or reproduced in any manner whatsoever without written permission except in the case of reprints in the context of reviews. For information, write Andrews McMeel Publishing, an Andrews McMeel Universal company, 4520 Main Street, Kansas City, Missouri 64111.

01 02 03 04 05 RDC 10 9 8 7 6 5 4 3 2 1

Library of Congress Cataloging-in-Publication Data

Joyce, Tim
    Life : the final frontier / Tim Joyce and Carl Kozlowski.
        p.   cm.
    ISBN 0-7407-1522-4 (pbk.)
    1. Conduct of life—Humor. I. Kozlowski, Carl.
II. Title.

PN6231.C6142J692001
818'.607—dc21

                                    2001022354

DESIGN AND COMPOSITION BY KELLY & COMPANY

─── **ATTENTION: SCHOOLS AND BUSINESSES** ───

Andrews McMeel books are available at quantity discounts with bulk purchase for educational, business, or sales promotional use. For information, please write to: Special Sales Department, Andrews McMeel Publishing, 4520 Main Street, Kansas City, Missouri 64111.

Carl wishes to dedicate this to all the Kozlowskis of Geronimo Circle (don't disown me!), as well as to Libby, Beth, and Laura, for making him believe he is funny.

Tim dedicates this to Tom, Joanne, and all the kids, as well as to Chris, Amanda, and Amy. Most of all he thanks God for Connie.

Tim and Carl also thank John Roy for being a guardian angel.

CONTENTS

Contents

ADDRESS TO THE GRADUATING CLASS

Ladies, gentlemen, and whatever else. We stand at the edge of the brink of a cliff on the ledge of a precipice overlooking a chasm that may well in fact be a void. Confronted as we are with a cavern of such great size we must act, and act, if not quickly, then at least in a manner one might refer to as moderately snappy. It is not enough to look at the hole before us, compare it to our ass, and move on . . . No! We must take immediate and perhaps even foolish action. This great emptiness must be turned at least into a landfill, or dug deeper, perhaps to China.

• X •

For you see, like an unexcused flatus, the past lies behind us, while the present sits like humidity all around. Which brings us to the future. The future . . . ahh yes, the future . . . We all must remember that the future is like that goddamned waitress at Denny's; you never know what it will bring. So we are left to ask: Will the future bring us the patty melt we requested? Or will it, like that lazy trumped-up scullery maid who took our order, bring us waffles instead? And if she does, will we find that we like the waffles? Confronted with the eventuality of all of these eventualities we must eventually take control of our fate, face the future, and withhold the tip.

For it is a real world we are off to face. Not the Real World we see on MTV but a really real world with real realities. So let us get real. We all must live our lives, at least until we die at which point you're on your own, buddy.

So what words of wisdom can I impart to you all as you face the future and pray the end of my speech is near so you can have at the punch and cookies the local Jaycees have so generously donated?

Well, let me first repeat the words a wise man said to me when I was your age. "Stay the hell off of my lawn!" How true I found those words to be when his Doberman caught me and noshed on my ass like a Steak-Umm. So let me repeat: Stay off of people's lawns for crissake! And would it kill you to wipe your feet and take out the garbage? Sheesh!

So I reach the point where I must conclude, for time waits for no man and I only put a quarter in the meter. Never forget the words I have said to you today, especially since I forgot to write them down and might need them repeated back to me over the phone at the County Jail. Always keep in mind the guiding philosophy of Victoria's Secret: "Life is what happens to you while you're busy making underpants."

Thank you all. God bless you, and that blessing goes double if anyone has sneezed recently . . .

INTRODUCTION

Hello, Dear Reader! Thank you for buying this book. May we suggest you purchase hundreds of copies and distribute them to every person you know on even the most casual basis?

Can't blame us for trying right off the bat.

There are two things we cherish as a society, the right to a happy childhood and the right to a death with dignity. Between that idyllic youth and untimely death there is the untidy business of living your life as an adult.

We've been staggering around this adult world for a lot of years now. We know some stuff. Trust us.

We know the likely path you will take in your life. We know . . . what a drag it is likely to be.

Nonetheless, here you are. You have graduated from school, whatever school that may be. Perhaps it is grad school, maybe it is college, or it could even be high school. Hell, for all we know you simply have been expelled from whatever institution has had its chairs subjected to the wear and tear from contact with your soft and soggy rump all these years.

Whatever your situation, and sad as it may be, you've had the wisdom to buy our book. Our desire is to help ease your transition into young adulthood, or as we like to call it, the "Pre-Failure Stage."

We are here to send you off into Life . . . The Final Frontier.

But first let us express our warm pride in you, our Dear Reader.

Congratulations, Graduate!!!

Read this book.

Learn it.

Know it.

Love it.

There will be a quiz at the end.

LIFE

THE FINAL FRONTIER

SECTION ONE

SEIZE THE DAY JOB

Section One is perhaps our favorite section of the book. Or perhaps it isn't really. Maybe it is just the weak material we want to get out of the way as big-time professional authors. You, Dear Reader, shall never know. It's better that way, believe you me.

In this, the first section, we will deal with the process of setting up your so-called career, although we suspect that the term "career" is stretching it a bit when it comes to describing what you will be doing to scrape together a living until you die.

CHAPTER ONE

YOUR CAREER:
THE ROADMAP TO LOSERVILLE

So, you've made the biggest mistake a student can make. You've left the comfort of the college campus to make something of yourself in the real world. For reasons only you can explain you have given up binge drinking, casual interdormitory romantic contact, and the credit card your mom and dad secured for you (with a deposit of a thousand dollars and to use "only in an emergency," which you interpreted as "only when you are out of money for pizza") to go off and make your mark.

Well, here is my advice . . .

Good heavens! Go back! Don't ever, ever, ever leave the cushy life of the undergraduate world. The real world is a hellhole! There are bills to pay! These bills must be paid (with the exception of a few aboriginal cultures) with money! You, graduate, must somehow *earn* that money! For the love of all that is holy stay in school forever!

You didn't take that last paragraph seriously, did you? Sigh . . . Don't say we didn't warn you.

You have to go get a job, my friend! Allow us to offer some words of advice.

First of all, you'll want to find a job in your chosen field. That could be one of a million possible fields of study offered by today's modern colleges, so let's look at just a few of these myriad pathways of matriculation. This is an unscientific survey of college majors, based on the geeks and pinheads with whom we associate.

• 5 •

IF YOU MAJORED IN ACCOUNTING

Congratulations! You chose a field in which people *actually find work!* Chances are you don't need my advice in finding a job. Therefore let me give you one small piece of post-employment advice: Never, ever, speak about your accounting job to anyone with whom you desire physical contact.

Just trust me on this one.

The advice for accounting goes for anything you may have majored in that required you to enter any building on campus where a business course was offered.

So let us move on to the bachelor's degrees that guarantee a fruitless employment search.

Let's talk about what I majored in . . .

THEATRE ARTS

Every college has a theatre department. No one knows why, really. It just seems that when the plans are drawn up for a college campus the architects and planners slip a performing arts building into the blueprints, and mysteriously, no one complains.

Well, now you've gone and done it! You went and studied acting in college. Shame on you! What did your parents ever do to you to deserve this?

For the newly graduated actor or actress here is some brief employment advice.

Simply stated, the hardest part of being an actor is learning the daily specials. It is also good to remember that you always serve from the left, and that the coffee cup should never be less than 50 percent full if you want a good tip.

"But I am a trained actor!" you may whine.

Yep. You are. And that's why you're working at a restaurant. I mean, think about it . . . they made you learn lines in the theatre department. Why? So you'd have no problem remembering the daily specials after graduation.

Oh, by the way, Theatre Major, you're in trouble when it comes to figuring out how to add up the checks—they didn't teach you any of that in voice and movement class.

I guess maybe you should have majored in accounting if you wanted to work as a waiter.

Let's move on.

Maybe you attended college on an athletic scholarship, which most likely means this book is being read aloud to you by someone else.

If you're a jock, then you majored in . . .

PHYSICAL EDUCATION

Don't tell me, Scholar Athlete; here's what made you pick this prestigious course of study:

In between reps on one of the shiny machines in the gym, this thought entered your mind: "Maybe I should have a backup plan."

It occurred to you that if somehow you didn't vault from collegiate sports stardom directly into the NBA, WNBA, NFL, WNFL, WWF, WWWF, NHL, WNHL, or the CIA, you would need something to fall back on.

You figured you could always work as a gym teacher.

Well, take a lap. You were wrong.

Sure there are about twenty-seven million grade schools, high schools, middle schools, and culinary schools out there, and they certainly do have gym teachers at all of those schools. But think about it. Remember the person who taught gym at your high school? What did he weigh, about 371 pounds? How old was he? About ninety-six?

Of course he was. That is because gym teachers never die.

Why? Because they never exercise; they just watch other people exercise.

That explains the fat pretty well when you think about it. Gym teachers never die and they are always balloons. It's a fact.

For instance . . . the man who taught me how to do jumping jacks in my youth also taught Teddy Roosevelt how to do them. My gym teacher (like the gym teacher of every person reading this book) is alive and well and taunting some terrified skinny kid.

Currently, that terrified kid is stuck halfway up a rope.

So Phys Ed Major, where do you go from here, you might ask?

It comes down to one of two quite noble professions really: furniture delivery or bouncer at a sports bar.

Yep. You'd better be ready to either wrestle drunken phys ed majors out of a tavern or heave a refrigerator up three flights of stairs. That's your *real* backup plan, Muscle Boy.

POLITICAL SCIENCE

If you majored in this particular area, perhaps you can explain something to me.

What in the name of God is going on here? As I sit in my cold-water flat typing madly into this laptop, I am a resident of a country in which a professional wrestler has gained national political prominence. Is that what our Founding Fathers intended when they wrote the Declaration of Independence, or the Constitution, or the Magna Carta, or whatever piece of scraggy brown paper (where the letter "S" really looks a lot like the letter "F") we are basing our government upon these days?

What gives, Mr. Big Shot Political Scientist? Political science? HA! More like political witchcraft these days.

Anyway, whatever "political science" is, you went ahead and studied it. Now you want a job in politics, I suppose. Even though I'm not inclined to help anyone head off into that direction, I believe I can in fact help.

Want to be in politics? That's easy! Walk out into the street, ask the first person you see what they want, then promise to give it to them.

Congratulations. You are now in politics.

Don't worry about actually following through on what you told the stranger you would get her or him. That's not the point of politics. The point is to get elected by any means necessary. So tell people exactly what they want to hear, no matter how stupid it is.

Here are a few easy things to say to the bone-heads who live in this country that are guaranteed to get them to punch the card (hopefully all the way through . . .) next to your name. All of these suggestions are, more or less, *actual political ideas* recently used by successful politicians. So, look directly into people's eyes and:

Tell them you will cut taxes but spend more.

Tell them you will spend less and get even more.

Tell them you will put a chicken in every pot.

Tell them you'll stash some pot in every chicken.

Tell them you intend to build a bridge into the Twenty-first Century.

Tell them there will be no toll on that bridge.

Tell them you'll give them 1,000 Points of Light, or better yet . . .

Tell them you'll pour them 1,000 Pints of Bud Light.

Tell them you will speak softly and carry a big stick, then . . .

Show them your big stick.

Tell them you'll invade some country where the army rides around on llamas.

People here love stuff like that.

Finally, just one word of warning: Don't have sex in your office.

Apparently, people here don't love stuff like that.

Nuclear Physics

Personally, I find it hard to believe that anyone capable of understanding the nuances and intense calculus that are the bread and butter precepts of nuclear science will be reading this book. But if you did, let me just say . . .

Good for you, Poindexter!

You will never lack for employment. The world needs nuclear physicists for the simple reason that the entire economy of the planet is based on the military-industrial complex. Stated simply, that means we need plenty of nuclear weapons all over the globe, and we need those weapons to be pointed at each other all of the time.

Otherwise, well . . . a lot of guys with really cool uniforms will be out of work.

And the people who write and report what those bomb-wielding guys in cool uniforms are doing will be out of work. And the people who construct the bombs that the bomb-wielding guys in cool uniforms point at each other will be out of work. And the people who wash up, store, and shine the bombs for the bomb-wielding guys in cool uniforms will be out of work.

In short, we will all be out of work if we ever get rid of all the nuclear bombs.

And if you as a socially conscious nuclear physicist cannot morally or ethically work for the military-industrial complex, don't worry. There is still plenty of work for you!

In the safe, sane, and well-regulated world of nuclear power.

How many times have you heard someone you admired referred to as a "Renaissance Man?" What does this really mean? Well, first and foremost, you should remember that the Renaissance occurred back in the years between 1350 and 1700, so apparently being a Renaissance Man involves having no electricity.

Here's a quick guide to being the next Leonardo da Vinci.

Be a Renaissance Man:

Throw your raw sewage out of the second-floor window.

Be a Renaissance Man:

Walk the streets of your town in tights and a codpiece.

Be a Renaissance Man:

Clean your teeth with a pointed stick.

Be a Renaissance Man:

Accuse your neighbors of witchcraft.

Be a Renaissance Man:

Annoy your parents by pursuing a career as a lute player.

Be a Renaissance Man:

Set off to discover the New World in a leaky wooden ship.

Be a Renaissance Man:

Conduct all correspondence via carrier pigeon.

Be a Renaissance Man:

Deny the existence of your electric bill.

Be a Renaissance Man:

Rob a grave and dissect the body.

There really is only one other course of study that bears mentioning in this book when it comes to entry-level employment tips, and that is:

COMPUTER SCIENCE

Chances are, if you majored in computer science, you didn't buy this book. Oh, you are reading this book all right; you just didn't buy it.

You downloaded it off of the Internet—for free. You didn't pay a cent for this book. But you are reading it nonetheless.

And now you want my advice.

Well take a hike, Nerd. I don't give out advice for free.

CHAPTER TWO

How to Hide Your Complete Unhireability

So, you've decided to enter the working world. Well, "decided" may not be the proper term; like most of us, you were dragged kicking and screaming into the land of the Nine-to-Fivers, who are actually a vanishing breed as employers these days demand ever longer hours and ever greater effort from their minions.

Your parents, unfortunately, have finally wised up and decided that they deserve to be treated better than the corner cash machine. Your friends have also been cut off and are in the same boat as you—there's no way you can keep bumming money off them. And somehow, you can't quite bring yourself to sit on a street corner with a change cup.

So here you are, reading this book as you take a much-needed break from the headache-inducing small type found in Sunday's job ads. You've already seen that every job that could possibly be worthwhile demands experience and a sense of *savoir faire.* You have to convince prospective employers that you are the man or woman for the job. But how do you do it?

Two simple, basic principles, culled from centuries of workplace tradition: lying and pretending.

Yes, prepare to engage in the most fanciful string of embellishments you will ever unleash upon your fellow man in this lifetime. It's time to prepare for the dreaded Job Interview.

THE PHONE INTERVIEW

The first step in preparing for the interview is the phone call inquiry about the job in question. Most job ads, of course, request that you don't inundate their office with calls. Ignore such pleas, for in fact, they are merely testing your sense of persistence and perseverance. Call, and call often, to show just how much you want to be their silly little wage slave. And if they tell you to buzz off, then you scratch them off your list and move on to the next prospect.

THE RÉSUMÉ

Once you make it past the phone interview, it's time to draft a résumé. The résumé is the piece of paper that introduces you to the world—make sure it's dramatic! This is your golden chance to reinvent yourself, to redress past grievances, and undo past wrongs!

You didn't work at 7-Eleven as a cashier last summer; why, you were a monetary engineer at a multinational corporation! Even if your work record consists exclusively of menial labor at convenience stores, you have the right to make it sound spectacular. For instance, if your coworkers were Pakistanis and Guatemalans, you can even put down "Experience with international relations" under the "interests" section of your curriculum vitae (that's fancy Latinspeak for résumé).

Just remember one thing about résumés: In these hectic times, no one has time to check them!

Do you really think that squat, balding middle manager in charge of interviewing your sorry ass is gonna bother to see if you attended Harvard? The answer is N-O, no! The corporate world is Darwinism at its finest: As long as that pathetic piece of management ranks above you, he doesn't care where you came from or what your human rights are.

Our personal favorite part of the résumé has to be "interests and hobbies." This is where you can really go to town, describing your black belt ninja-level powers of *ninjitsu,* describing your harrowing climb on Mt. Everest, or listing the thirty-seven languages you've mastered to compete in the modern global marketplace.

Sure, you're lying, but who's gonna have the guts to call you on it? Once you receive that inevitable call to come in for an interview, just lean back and offer your fake pearls of wisdom at any given opportunity. The more impressive your anecdotes, the more control you'll have in the process. Within moments, they'll be skipping the usual battery of questions and moving directly into salary negotiations!

THE INTERVIEW

So now that you've described yourself as a world-class player, what should you wear to the special occasion? Well, realize the only day you will ever feel *more* uncomfortable is your wedding day, and dress accordingly. Ladies, a bridal gown minus the train will suffice. Men, sport a tuxedo.

But don't fret: You'll never have to dress like this for the office again, because nowadays *every* day is a casual day in American business.

So, what do you say now that you're actually *in* the interview? Know, first of all, that you will likely be hermetically sealed in this stranger's office for a good forty-five minutes to an hour. (That is, unless you're applying at Wendy's).

You want to attract the interviewer's attention, without overdoing it. If you sound too confident, capable, or available, you'll run the risk of doubling your interview time to an excruciating two hours. And note that while you might liken such an experience to your final exam in college, you cannot chew gum, pick your nose, or fart at any time during the interview.

The two words the interrogator is waiting to hear are "teamwork" and "deadline." Much like profanity is used in an urban milieu, these words can be applied as nouns, adjectives, verbs, or adverbs. Try, however, to use "teamwork" and "deadline" in the context of a sentence, or you'll run the risk of sounding like a Tourette's victim.

Another valuable skill in the new global economy is bilingualism. But fear not—claiming knowledge of Spanish is easier than you think! You understand the phrase *"Yo quiero Taco Bell,"* don't you? Congratulations, you're fluent!

Finally, be sure to stare blankly at the interviewer the entire time. It'll give him the added challenge of reading your mind and emotions. And besides, if you get the job, you'll be staring blankly at your computer and coworkers for the next forty years so it'll be good practice.

CHAPTER THREE

TEMPING (OR: HOW TO BE A WHORE WITHOUT TAKING YOUR CLOTHES OFF)

Let's face it—work sucks.

First of all, most of you have to physically leave your homes to get to work each day. That means, in order to earn a living, you have to get out of bed and switch off the television set (the horror!) before sharing a ride to work on public transportation with a bunch of other disgruntled strangers you wouldn't choose to meet at a haunted house. And, if you're lucky enough to control your environment and select your travel companions or lack thereof, by driving a car, you'll still have to put up with the road rage and general driving incompetence of the six million people around you.

Once at the workplace, you will have to pretend to be productive for at least eight hours a day. Memos will be tossed at you, bosses will scream at you, and you'll feel like nobody knows you are a dignified person of worth. And these days, things are worse than ever. At least in the past, your $20,000-a-year job was a starting point to rise from, and if you played your cards right with a company you could tolerate, you could just climb the pointless corporate ladder forever.

Sure, having a job is tough, but if you like to eat, you have to accept a steady job as a necessary evil. Or do you? There is actually another way, a way to get your hand into an employer's pocket without handing over your heart and soul . . . Behold the glamorous and nomadic life of The Temp!

Temps are essentially corporate gigolos. They get paid by the hour to fulfill client needs. And if they've got the right skill set (computer rather than sexual abilities are generally required), they can make up to $14 an hour answering phones, making pointless copies, and mastering PC-based video games. The upside is that employers think of temps as invisible creatures unworthy of acknowledgment, thereby excluding them from the highly personal abuse reserved for their full-time drones.

The following are handy steps to keep the temp worker sane.

1. Learn what to say, and what not to say, while temping.

You can get away with just about anything as a temp since no one's ever seen you before and, chances are, won't see you again. So be creative!

Here's an example of catchy conversation, although the lasting impression you make may not be a positive one:

EXEC: There's a lot of people out today.
TEMP: Must be recovering from the weekend.
EXEC: Yep, it seems that way.
TEMP: And I know how they feel! I got so bombed I had to go to the emergency room! WOO!

Or:

EXEC: Lainie's out sick today.
TEMP: I just got over a little infection myself. Thank God for penicillin, eh?

2. Learn to do creative accounting.

Figure how much you can get by on in a month and work just enough to hit that minimum. See if you can meet the challenge you set for yourself and learn to stay within your financial boundaries.

For instance, thanks to an incredible rental deal, my bare-minimum expenses for survival come out to $570 a month. That means I have to work just

seven and a half days a month to make the money
I need to survive. Whooeee!

3. Create your own benefits package.

No one is looking out for you now that you're in the
real world. And do you really understand or care
about HMOs or your 401(k) anyway? So why not
focus on the things you really can use in your daily
life? Seize the moment! Find the supply closet!

Secondly, if they say go to the bathroom any-
time, or drink as many sodas as you want, *take them
up on their offer!* This doesn't happen in full-time
corporate America, and this is the closest you'll
ever get to perks. So stuff your face, drown your
sorrows in coffee, and pee like crazy!

You should also be able to take care of all your
long-distance calling needs while getting paid. That's
a commodity more valuable than a 401(k). Think
drawing 8 percent interest a year is as satisfying as
thirty minutes yakking with your friend in New
York on the company WATS line? Fuhgeddaboutit!

Sure, Sprint offers rates of ten cents a minute. How about zero?!

Temps can also receive free computer training, an unexpected bonus offered by agencies to make them think that you're suddenly gonna be worth an extra five bucks per hour on the open market. You'll only see a fifty-cent raise on your paycheck, but they'll be pocketing nine times that for every hour you work.

But hey, look on the bright side—it's still better than shelling out a thousand bucks per class at Mac University. So, if you need to brush up your computer skills, head on down to your temp agency and keep your money for booze. By the end of each Friday, you're gonna need it.

4. But what about medical benefits?

What's better for the psyche than the knowledge that you may not ever have to face your boss and coworkers again? Imagine experiencing that thrill every day.

Choosing your own workdays leads to a loss of stress and enables you to acquire a healthy tan in the summer or to curl up under the covers for days at a time in the winter. You'll soon find a decrease in headaches, ulcers, depression, and other forms of mental illness to go with the decrease in your financial status and credit worthiness.

Equally healthy is enjoying a movie in the middle of the traditional workday—or heck, see two (don't forget, it's more simple and cost-effective than ever to enjoy a bonus film in the age of the multiplex!). You can also go jogging and shopping (well, window shopping—you'll have a tight budget to stick to as you're only making temp wages).

5. Expand your mind.

You and your fellow temps all have overpriced yet practically worthless liberal arts degrees, so don't let that knowledge go to waste! Play on the sympathies of a fairly young boss and drag a day's work into a weeklong assignment. You can talk about everything with your fellow temps, from the Meese Commission Study of Pornography to the latest baseball trades and the theme of paranoia in mass entertainment, creating a discussion panel that would put ABC's *Politically Incorrect* to shame.

There's one agency in Chicago that actually maintains a paid stand-by policy offering another great opportunity for a daily discussion group. You come in at 8:30 A.M. merely hoping to find work, and if there is none, you get to go home at 11:00. So you'll get paid four hours at your regular rate (up to $12 an hour, so that's nearly forty bucks!) just to sit there for two and a half hours! You can engage in a twentysomething version of *The Breakfast Club,* commiserating with your fellow losers in life about how you got there, asking why didn't people talk you out of studying drama or English (your native tongue), and well, your own personal issues.

You can make up the rest of the $30 you've lost by not getting a full day's work by hanging out in Borders, hiding out in a downstairs chair and reading every magazine that remotely interests you.

After all, the best thing about hanging out in a book-store is learning things you'd never know otherwise. For example, stash *Libido: The Journal of Human Sensuality* inside *Time* magazine to hide your embar-rassment while reading about the latest trends in nipple rings.

Oh yeah, even if you get stuck working all day, you can still read at most temp jobs. Just don't kick up your heels, plant 'em on top of your desk, and draw attention to yourself. Keep your head low and be discreet, which is good training for when you graduate/move on to the utterly fulfilling world of a full-time job.

6. Leave a legacy.

As we discussed earlier, you can get away with a lot as a temp. So feel free to improve your dating life and build your self-confidence in approaching poten-tial dates by scamming on women or men in each workplace, because you'll never see them again (unless you *really* get lucky). Besides if they shoot you down, who cares? You're temping, so your life's in a nihilistic freefall anyway.

Feel a need to do something worthwhile at each workplace? Then sample one of every type of soda in their fridge, and then suggest a recycling program as your day's major contribution.

There are plenty of other ways to make sure they'll always remember your sorry ass, ranging from poor phonework to bad typing to shouting out your own contributions to executives' conversations as they pass by. Just remember to keep the "temp" in temping—nobody wants to name it as their job on their tax forms.

Just Passing Through:
The Insider Files of a Chicago Temp

While most temp assignments will render you as anonymous as the second gunman in Dealey Plaza, putting you through eight hours a day of stultifying stupidity, there are a few choice companies that can almost make temping feel worthwhile. The more famous the company name, the greater your chances of learning some top-secret information you can sell for fun and profit.

Here's a behind-the-scenes glimpse of four of America's most prominent temp employers, as experienced in their Chicago branch offices:

a) Sara Lee. This is a great place to start your temping career (er, I mean experience . . .). An "all the pastries you can eat" policy greeted me on my first day in the temp world, making me feel that yes, indeed, I had made a smart choice after all. Benefits, schmenefits! I was eating five types of pastry for free!

Sara Lee employees get those every morning, along with an all-day, unlimited supply of every type of soda known to man, stocked in perfect formation in the fridge. Oh, deluxe bottled waters, too! Plus, so little actual work that by the end of the day, you may not only question the need for a temp there but also the purpose of your very existence.

Just keep jamming those sugars down your throat. It'll all be okay.

b) Leo Burnett. The Nirvana of temp assignments, this advertising agency giant has an all-casual, all-the-time approach to officewear. One friend of mine wears shorts, a baseball cap, and a three-day growth of beard to work in the morning. And attention all nicotine junkies: people smoke at will here because this is the place that invented the Marlboro Man!

All the Coke, Cherry Coke, Diet Coke, Sprite, and Rambling Root Beer you can drink shoots out of dispensers as fast as you can drink it because they handle Coke, too! Plus, free red apples for eating abound, and you get to work for people who spend their days watching music videos in search of the next great ad tune and the next big director.

You'll be laughing at both the incredibly light workload and the sound of that VW da da da song blasting out of your assigned boss's office. In fact, I'd like to thank Leo Burnett for subsidizing the writing of this chapter.

c) Arthur Andersen. The most demonic workplace of all for temps, as you're subjected to crushing boredom without any of the accoutrements you can find in most temp places. The halls are so quiet you can hear the cooling system emanating almost silently from the walls.

People don't talk to each other here, instead staring up at the ceiling blankly wondering how they ever allowed themselves to work in a Dilbert-like setting, their entire world encompassed by the cloth-walled cubicle around them. Just like a terrorist's hostage, when I had nothing to do, I still wasn't allowed to read. So I read surreptitiously, beneath the desk.

They busted me, and proceeded to violate at least one tenet of the UN Declaration of Human Rights by conjuring up a thousand-page binder with multicolored pages and asking me to make another one like it within the hour. On one of my days there, I met a half-insane female temp who said she'd temped at various Andersen desks for a month and a half without ever having an actual task to repeat.

Arthur Andersen offers the ultimate glory and disgrace all in one, as you live the dream of being paid to do nothing, and the nightmare of feeling your brain turn to jelly. But one woman I filled in for had more desk computer games than anyone I'd ever seen, stopping just shy of having a desktop Nintendo 64. At least I managed to learn the Minesweeper game by noon.

d) *Chicago Tribune.* Ah, yes! Experience the rush of the newsroom and feel the sheer excitement of being at Ground Zero as the latest developments of life across Planet Earth come hurtling in to be dissected and digested by self-appointed media "experts" seeking to help the unwashed millions of newspaper readers grasp a minor understanding of life around them.

Be the first on your block to hear the latest updates on presidential impeachment scandals! Catch the latest photographs of people in misery (always a staple of local news coverage)!

Granted, all this *sounds* exciting. But alas,

if you're a mere temp, editors at the *Chicago Tribune*—or any other paper with competent leadership at the helm—won't allow you anywhere near the good stories. Instead, you'll be trapped like I was, collecting press release faxes filled with breathless prose, each seeking to catch the attention of the paper's gossip columnists.

In my two days of service to the "Inc." column, I found myself chasing down five sets of faxes from one elite men's clothier alone. As the store's PR flack begged me to find and pass on their allegedly vital information, I finally came across the pearl of wisdom they wished to share with the public: Vice President Al Gore had stopped in for a visit and praised their selection of ties.

Filled with the satisfaction that indeed there were other workers forced to be even bigger whores than I was, my time at the newspaper passed all too quickly. The one other press release that stood out in my mind came from the set of the film *U.S. Marshals,* which proclaimed that career drug felon/actor Robert Downey Jr. was behaving impeccably and soberly on their set.

As I strolled quickly through the halls en route to dropping that item off, I realized that I was, for one brief moment, a part of the never-ending cycle of celebrity pseudo-journalism that passes these days for serious news. And I felt great!

While this may not be the Pulitzer-winning experience you had hoped for, it still offers the tawdry thrill of working at the *National Enquirer* while drawing a paycheck from a venerable journalistic institution. And the best part is, no one ever has to know what you really did within the walls of Tribune Tower. For all they know, you caught the president with his pants down.

CHAPTER FOUR

FIRST JOBS OF
FAMOUS PEOPLE

By now, every person alive on the planet Earth has become familiar with Andy Warhol's prediction that each human being will be famous for at least fifteen minutes. In fact, sad to say, Andy is more famous for that quote than he is for the paintings that made him a quotable famous person in the first place. Admit it, Dear Reader; you have no idea what Andy Warhol originally became famous for, do you?

Don't feel bad. Almost no one does. Apparently it had something to do with soup.

What is, in fact, important to note is that he made his "fame" prediction back in the 1960s . . . that's right, the 1960s. That would be that godforsaken decade your parents (or even grandparents) just cannot seem to shut up about or get over. The Age of Aquarius . . .

When "X" was a letter that came after "Malcolm" not "Generation."

Too bad no one has ever written any books about the 1960s, or movies, or television shows.

Whatever . . .

The fact is, the standards of fame these days are very different from forty, thirty, or even five years ago.

Back in the Age of Aquarius, it wasn't as easy to be famous. You had to actually *do* something—like write a book, or invent a vaccine, or star in a movie.

Or at least brandish a weapon at an elected official.

Thank heavens nowadays becoming a household name isn't all that much work. Thanks to Jerry,

Ricki, Jenny, Judge Judy, and the World Wrestling Federation, all you have to do to become famous in the postmodern era is have absolutely no sense of shame whatsoever.

It's that easy!

Let the world know that you come from a long line of transvestite vampires! (Heck, you won't even be the first to admit that one.) Just make sure the VCR is rolling so you can show the grandkids what you looked like in drag, as well as what you looked like having a chair slammed over your head.

What magic moments . . .

Even so, there are probably many of you out there who want to become rich and famous the "old-fashioned" way. So as a means of providing you with inspiration in achieving your goal of well-earned fame, let's look at the lives of some famous people throughout history and see where they started when they first entered the workforce.

ATTILA THE HUN

It's a well-documented fact that as a teenager Attila was quite lazy, spending most of his time sitting on the couch reading comic books until his father told him he had to cut his hair and get a job. Not wanting to give up his ankle-length locks or the beard he had been growing since age two, Attila got a job as a pizza delivery boy. It is believed that this experience gave him the inspiration to go house to house for a living when he became a man, often with the promise that he would sack your town within thirty minutes or the entire raid would be free.

ABRAHAM LINCOLN

The life of Abe Lincoln, or Honest Abe as he was known at the local pool hall, was a great example to us all. From his Gettysburg Address, which provided the nation with the promise of a "New Birth of Freedom," to his death at the hands of John Wilkes Booth, which provided us all with a good excuse to avoid seeing musical theatre, Abraham Lincoln was the epitome of American greatness.

What few Americans know was that Abe was also perhaps the first street mime in recorded history, a first job he undertook with honesty and vigor until, in an attempt to find a career more hated than mime, he studied to become a lawyer.

ELEANOR ROOSEVELT

Eleanor Roosevelt was more than just the wife of FDR. She was perhaps one of the greatest campaigners for both civil rights and the cause of women in the twentieth century.

Almost no one is aware that she first entered the workforce as a member of the long forgotten and short-lived "Women's Professional Kick-Boxing Association," which flourished for a brief period between the hours of seven and nine P.M. on October 27, 1939. After this 120-minute-long "Golden Age" of women's kick-boxing, the league was disbanded, largely due to a lack of attendance, participants, or interest on the part of anyone who was reasonably sober that night. Despite this setback she did retire undefeated, having successfully kicked Herbert Hoover's wife, Tillie, really hard in the shins.

THE TELETUBBIES

Fuzzy, chubby, and strangely unintelligible, the Teletubbies speak to the children of the world every day from the screens of their television sets. What happy, furry, and loving little asexual lumps they are! There's Tinky Winky, Dipsy, LaLa, and of course who could ever forget the enigmatic Po? But before they entranced us all with their bulbous electronic hijinks, what did these four adorable sweetie pies do for a living?

I'll tell you what they did, pal. They were highly paid assassins for the Central Intelligence Agency, that's what! Oh, yeah. You thought Dipsy was cute? Think again. Dipsy was the last person ever to see Jimmy Hoffa alive. You wonder why Tinky Winky gets Jerry Falwell all upset? Maybe it's because old

Tinky has some photos the Reverend would like to see destroyed. Have you ever wondered why LaLa never talks about where he was the day JFK was shot?

And then there's Po . . . Happy happy little Po . . . How did little Po ever get his or her name? Hmmm. Let's just see. Who lives in the Vatican? The Po Ntiff . . . Can't believe that the largest church in the western world is run by a sweaty actor in a suit? Refuse to acknowledge this obvious fact? Well think a minute. Have you ever seen Po and the Pope in the same room?

Makes you think, don't it?

O. J. SIMPSON

Before the Juice became the first American to combine constant daily golfing with criminal investigating, he was rumored to have been a football player or something. No one really knows for sure, but we do know that his first employment came as a door-to-door representative of the Ginsu Knife Company.

Still don't want to take the easy way? Do you still need inspiration to achieve greatness?

Well then, here is a quick and easily read list for you . . .

Famous people and their first job

Famous Person	First Job
Dan Quayle	Doorjamb
Madonna	Jerry Falwell's Receptionist
Dennis Rodman	Marriage Counselor
Ted Koppel	Rodeo Clown
Bill Gates	Sex Therapist
Britney Spears	Prison Guard
John the Baptist	Professional Accordion Player
General Robert E. Lee	Flamenco Dance Instructor
Joan of Arc	Firewood Saleswoman
King Tutankhamen	Cage Cleaner, Cairo Zoo
Barbara Walters	Speech Pathologist
Janet Reno	Lingerie Model

CHAPTER FIVE

BASIC AUTO MAINTENANCE (OR: WHY YOUR MECHANIC MAKES MORE THAN YOU DO)

Have you ever driven your car away from the auto shop and had the uneasy feeling that the entire staff there was laughing like hyenas at you behind your back? That is a common feeling, and there is a simple reason why you think that.

They are.

"But why?" you may ask, "Why are they having a laugh at my expense?" The explanation for that is pretty easy, my friend, and deep down inside you probably already know it. Let us set the time machine back a few years and look at things as they were when you were in high school.

Chances are you thought you were pretty darned smart back in high school. Remember? You were on the debate team, the yearbook staff, you may even have been the valedictorian of your senior class. Your parents were so proud they gave you a car. They helped you take care of it. Then you went to college and really wowed 'em.

Wow.

But before we move on, let's go back to high school . . . Remember that guy who took all the shop classes? Remember his friends? What was it you called them, Motor Heads? Grease Monkeys? Wrench Jockeys?

Boy did you ever look down on them! Ha Ha Ha! Look at the shop guys! Losers!

Admit it—that's what you thought. But now you're fresh out of school. On your own. With your own car. Your own used car, that is. Funny how life works.

See, Mom and Dad aren't going to pay for the repairs now that you've struck out on your own. So guess who's laughing now? That's right, Smartypants . . . all those guys you looked down on in high school.

Admit it—when you take that car into the shop you feel as dumb as a brine shrimp. When the man in the coveralls looks at you and gestures back at your disabled transportation, you haven't got the vaguest idea what he is talking about, do you?

Be honest.

If you are the average person you wouldn't know a catalytic converter if there was one floating in your soup. That's why you'll happily pay the "dumbest kid" in your high school class to fix it. See, he would know the catalytic converter if it was floating in your soup.

So who's the dumb kid now, Mr. Philosophy Major?

While you wait in the repair shop for the former dumb kid to tell you what's causing your eleven-year-old dorkmobile to spew black smoke and sputter like a Cub Scout at a nude beach, perhaps you might want to check the walls of the repair shop. Go ahead, look at the sign that lists their labor rate . . . Look at it!

No, no, you didn't read it wrong, Einstein. It says $75 an hour. Seventy-five dollars!

Even your psychiatrist doesn't charge that. And without your car, you can't even go see your psychiatrist. In fact, it's not unlikely that you will see your psychiatrist in the waiting room of the repair shop as well. See, he doesn't know what a catalytic converter is either.

The hour and a half you wait for the mechanic to return from the bay and tell you what's wrong with your car is the longest ninety minutes you will ever spend. You'll try to distract yourself by reading the three-year-old copies of *Sports Illustrated* they've thoughtfully left for you. Maybe you'll buy a can of pop. Perhaps you'll treat yourself to a gumball. If the repair shop is nice they'll even have free coffee for the patrons. Go ahead! Have a cup of java on the boys in the bay! At seventy-five bucks an hour they can afford it.

Finally, after half a pot of the strongest coffee this side of Istanbul, the mechanic will come out and call your name. If you're smart you won't answer. You'll run for your life.

He's about to start telling you why you have to give him five hundred dollars.

He'll start with the phrase, "Well, we checked the engine on the computer and this is what the problem is . . ." That's the last thing he'll say that you will understand at all.

Except the five hundred dollar part.

He will ramble on about the alternator fan belt or the fuel injectors or the overhead cams. All the while your eyes will glaze over. You will have absolutely no idea what he is talking about.

He will know that you have absolutely no idea what he is talking about. But he'll keep on talking about parts that he is about to replace in your car . . .

and you'll nod. He will take an eternity to get to the only part of the conversation you really care about anyway.

The part about the five hundred dollars.

All along you will both know that you are giving him the money. But he'll make you wait.

Why does he make you wait? Why does he torture you like this?

Because you asked for it, buster. You deserve every second of torture he dishes out. You owe him that five hundred bucks, even if all that's wrong with your car is that it's out of gas.

Why do you owe him? Because you wasted all that time in high school and college learning philosophy. And mocking him.

He knew you thought he was dumber than you. He wasn't. All along he was plotting this day of sweet revenge in his grease monkey mind. You will gladly pay restitution to him for your arrogance, restitution in the form of five hundred bucks. Your psychiatrist will pay him the same restitution as well.

It's a good lesson in humility when you think about it . . . I guess that's why "kar" is the first syllable in "karma."

Thus endeth the lesson, but, since you will inevitably face a mechanic who knows you know nothing at all about your car, here's a short list of parts that your car does not have. Hopefully this will save you embarrassment, if not money.

Your car does *not* have a:

Defibrillator

Blinker Fluid Reservoir

Carbuncle

Ionic Transmographier

Time Portal

Solar Interferometer

Starter Pistol

Irradiator

Clown Vent

Catatonic Converter

Aorta

Snooze Alarm

Proton Torpedo Valve

Picnic Gasket

Litter Box

Maypole

Crisper

Mine Sweeper

Semiautomatic Transmission

Martin Landau Roof

Cheese Filter

Electric Slide

Serling Rod

Big Bad Voodoo Daddy

Jimmy Hat

Iambic Pentameter

CHAPTER SIX

How to Hide the Fact That You're a Miserable Failure

Take a look around any bookstore. (Yes, feel free to even look now, as you consider your purchase of this book—*just make sure you buy this book!*)

You will find countless guides on how to achieve success. This is all well and good for those who dream of joining the Bill Gateses and Tony Robbinses of the world. But why are there no guides for the rest of us, or books on how to cope with our staggering failures?

Everyone deserves the answers to life's most humbling questions:

How do you live with yourself? And how do you hide your status from others? It may take a bit of hard work—and a lot of cleverness—but we're here to help.

First off, failure is a state of mind. Like Carl, you may be nearing thirty while driving the same car you had in college. While that might spell "loser" to you (and frankly, to most other casual observers), he prefers to confuse people and sound cool by calling his car "retro."

It's all in the semantics, people. While Carl is two steps away from bankruptcy on a financial level, he is almost foolishly happy. For he has attained the satisfaction you can't buy, that of accepting jobs where he is not a cog in the corporate wheel, but rather, blissfully free of nearly any and all responsibility.

That is the type of job you should be looking for. You can learn how to attain that kind of job in other chapters of this book. Here, we are merely helping you come up with the excuses for "what went wrong" in the eyes of the petty, small-minded people with whom you have to deal.

YOUR PARENTS (OR: THE FAMILY GESTAPO)

Ah, your parents. After raising you under their roof for at least eighteen years and paying for your college education, they may feel entitled to answers about your life choices and standard of living.

Frankly, they're right. But that doesn't mean you have to give them *true* answers.

There is one factor that plays in your favor when hiding the miserable wreck your life has become: not having children. You see, when you're childless, they never show any interest in actually coming to see you. But the moment you spawn rugrats, they'll be inventing holidays and birthdays to drop by.

So until you get that first big break, don't have that first big baby.

Secondly, this means you only have to visit your parents at times you select, or—like most people—at the holidays. At these festive times, they are more likely to blind themselves to any of your problems and adopt that happy holiday mantra: "We're together! Aren't the holidays *great*?!"

When you do go to visit your parents, adopting a more lavish persona should come easily. First off, replace your car. Sure, you may not be able to afford a new car and the bank may even laugh at you when you hit them up for a loan, but that's why the rental car industry is your godsend: even if you're the poorest man on Earth, you can afford almost any luxury automobile for three days at a time.

Suddenly, you'll be pulling up to the family homestead in a brand new BMW. Won't they be proud?

Third, borrow at least one nice suit from your friends, and then talk a friend into being your holiday date. This is, of course, designed to prevent your family from questioning your sexuality as well as your basic appeal to the rest of the human race.

Construct elaborate tales of your wonderful life together; after all, if you truly can't stomach each other, you can always believably "break up" right before Valentine's Day.

CLASS REUNIONS (OR: THE NEXT WORST THING TO SEEING YOUR PARENTS)

High school and college reunions are even more devastating than a visit to your parents. Here, you're going to have to be up close and personal with people who won't turn a blind eye to your heaving gut or rickety jalopy. These are people with no stake in your future or concern for your hopeless present.

They are the people who likely gave you wedgies and laughed at your, ahem, size in the locker room and turned you down for dates to the big dance. Oh boy, high school! Can't wait to go back and relive the memories!

The only reason to go back to your high school is either to wave your unexpected success in the face of your former tormentors (i.e., Bill Gates), or to see if you can relight a spark with a former fling and get lucky all weekend. Carl didn't attend his reunion because he has yet to achieve any quantifiable success in the outside world, and because he went to an all-boys Catholic school and therefore never had the privilege of having a fling in the first place.

Tim, however, attends all his reunions because he has gone on to be a nationally televised comedian (cool job) and he's married to his high school sweetheart. In other words, he has nothing to hide.

To make it through the reunion weekend, remember to follow the same principle you applied with your parents: Lie, and lie like you've never lied before. This doesn't mean, of course, that you lie without any skill or craftiness; rather, it means you invent a detailed history of your homes (yes, plural homes . . . you're not a loser, are you?!).

Talk at length about the ample nonexistent accomplishments of your nonexistent kids. Regale them with the story of how you and your fake wife met. (The fake story, of course! Not the tale of how you hired her from an escort service!) And settle back into your impeccably tailored suit borrowed from your much more successful buddy back home, smile glisteningly at every piece of dinner conversation, and try to hold back the tears—the tears that would reveal your true self.

ALUMNI MAGAZINES (OR: LEARNING THAT PEOPLE YOU HATE HAVE BETTER LIVES THAN YOU'LL EVER HAVE)

The college alumni magazine is an egregious display of boasting, built solely around the foolhardy idea that people want to hear about your success thirty years after you peed on the school mascot as part of your fraternity initiation ritual.

The problem for those of us who have yet to attain any success in the material world is that we have nothing to boast about in return. While you will always read about guys named Chet who just bought their second Gulfstream personal jet, married a supermodel, and live on a lavish offshore estate, you'll never see anyone write in with the staggering truth of far too many lives:

> "William Russell ('93) has settled into a long life of bored mediocrity with his thoroughly average job as a manager at Hardee's, with his thoroughly average wife, Trudy, and his sadly below-average children, Billy and Susie. They live in a thoroughly nondescript ranch house on the outskirts of Kansas City, and look forward to sharing decades of bored, apathetic lovemaking and stilted conversation until God mercifully sets them free from their average, mediocre lives."

So what do you do to make yourself feel better? You lie, of course. You dream up your fantasy lifestyle and set it on paper. And then you send in your own glorious entry in the annals of your school's folklore. Make yourself look downright fantastic! Who's gonna bother fact-checking your life?

> "William Russell ('93) has traveled the world as the lead ringmaster for the Ringling Bros. Circus, consoling himself for the loss of his romance with Claudia Schiffer by losing himself in the arms of the most beautiful women at each stop on his tour. Rather than confining himself to the smelly train travel of his fellow performers and underlings, he races from town to town in his shiny new 2000 Jaguar, realizing that its perfectly burnished hood will bring him far more satisfaction than the sniveling children of his university classmates."

There. That felt better, didn't it? And remember, it's only really a lie if you get caught.

CHAPTER SEVEN

The Final Truth About Work

So now you've learned just how rewarding a good lie can be: It can enhance your reputation, boost your self-esteem, and win the love and affection of both family and strangers. However, we need you to keep in mind one important but sad fact: The world will throw its own lies right back at you. Keep your eyes and ears wide open, because the less careful you are in life, the harder you'll actually have to work.

Work is a brainwashing process that begins in kindergarten, when we're forced to color inside the lines of a drawing. By the time we're done with high school, we're "showing our work" on every test or math problem we face. It's sad but true—before we know it, we become defined by our jobs, our status, or our lack thereof. Work has taken over our lives, wholly and completely.

"What do you do for a living?" "Where do you work?" "What's your j-o-b?" Our jobs tell us where we can live, how well we can eat, how extravagantly we can entertain ourselves. In fact, the word "work" is so insidious that it's even crept into the lexicon used in our nonwork activities.

Hell, we live in Chicago, "the city that works." We say our girlfriends are "working it" when they are being sassy or sexy. When we exercise, we "work out." And when we fight with our loved ones, we hope we can "work things out." We call streetwalkers "working girls," and trick ourselves into believing that the stripper in front of us is "working her way through college."

Politicians fight each election to prove how much they care about "the working man." And when we die, they sometimes say, "They worked themselves to the bone."

Some things shouldn't be work: eating good food, having good sex, watching a good movie. Yet someone's worked on preparing your meal, your lover is working to make sure you have a good time, and nearly five hundred people worked hard to make *Titanic* an enjoyable movie. (Just 'cause I didn't like it doesn't mean they didn't work hard.)

So for the love of God, the next time I'm at a restaurant, I beg of the waitstaff: Don't ask me "Are you still working on this?" as you try to clear my food and insinuate I've had more than enough chow. No, I *haven't* finished "working" on this; in fact, despite my gut, eating isn't my full-time job, but rather a highly enjoyable hobby.

Sad to say and shocking to believe, work is everywhere now. In fact, it sneaked up on most of us. When we were told we were gonna get paid $20,000 a year someday just for working, we thought it was the greatest deal in the world. Of course, we didn't understand that we were wage whores, or hamsters running in an endless Habitrail performing tasks beyond comprehension for unseen bosses with impenetrable agendas.

I ask you: Does it really require three people— including a senior executive—to form a consensus about which line of text a form letter should be folded upon?

No, it doesn't!

But if you're part of the working world, chances are you don't know better anymore because your mental faculties have been sapped by the alien tentacles of your company's management.

And look at the people around you—on the bus or train going to or from work, in your carpool, or worst of all, your lameass coworkers—and realize that you are spending more than fifty hours a week, *minimum,* with these chumps, all the while peppering your conversations with scintillating references to *Survivor* and how wonderful your hair or your shoes look.

And people wonder why postal workers whip out guns on occasion. Work has become the meaning of life . . . so why is it so often meaningless? Perhaps it seems meaningless because deep down it really is. And someday we'll evolve beyond a society and lifestyle in which we give our time and effort to those more powerful than us in exchange for pay that can never match our true, soul-stirring needs.

We'll be called to rise up and take arms in a show of force against those who oppress us in the name of commerce! We'll shake both our fists and our fannies as we march forward into a new day in which the lowly, peon, slave-wage–earning worker will—at last, at last!—be treated with respect!

I truly believe this in my heart. But knowing my general lack of effort and transposing it to anyone shiftless enough to read this book, I also realize that transformation ain't never gonna happen. Besides, they already tried it in Russia and look where it got them.

Oh, what's the use . . . just pass me an Old Style and let me recline in my La-Z-Boy in peace.

SECTION TWO

SEIZING YOUR
DAY-TO-DAY
MEDIOCRITY

You should have a job by the time you've read this far in our delightful book. But, Dear Reader, even you know that is not enough to make a human being out of you. You need to incorporate the accoutrements and habits of adulthood into your day-to-day life. In short, you need to learn how to live without accidentally killing yourself or inspiring those around you to kill you on purpose. Like any good pet, you need to be domesticated.

CHAPTER EIGHT

~~~~~

MOVING,
ROOMMATES,
AND YOU

So you've graduated from high school or college now. No doubt your parents have shared their heartfelt congratulations with you, as well as a note asking you to get out of their house permanently. We understand—it happens to all of us. Even Jesus had to hit the road when He was thirty.

But this can be a confusing time. You're off to meet new friends, leaving old ones behind, and trying to achieve a delicate balance in your relationship with your parents.

After all, you don't want them to realize you think of them as your personal loan officers, while they're trying to figure out a way to discreetly keep meddling with your life even as you move thousands of miles away from them (trust us, you'll want to).

You may think that the transition from college to independent life will be an easy step. It won't be, because on your road to academic enlightenment, you've forgotten one basic principle:

No matter how many times you protested for a free Tibet in college, or how proudly you displayed your copy of *Zen and the Art of Motorcycle Maintenance* on your dorm room bookshelf, you have no doubt succumbed to your Western materialistic traditions and collected a ton of crap in your time on this planet.

One day you will come to regret this.

This day is called Moving Day. U-Haul likes to call moving "The Great American Adventure." If moving is truly considered an adventure these days, then our standards are definitely slipping. Wrestling a wild crocodile with your bare hands is adventure, my friends. Spearing a feral, rabid boar on the points of its own tusks . . . that's adventure!

Moving is not an adventure. It's, well, pathetically boring and usually reserved for us poor saps who lack the funds to hire others to handle the nasty chore for them. This "adventure" consists of desperately calling in favors from every poor schmuck you've ever met, roping them into helping you carry the boxes, the glassware, and especially the couches up and down and around the impossibly narrow corners of dormitory and urban apartment staircases. For at least eight consecutive hours, your communication will consist of grunts, mutterings of that most pointless phrase—"Careful!"—and so much swearing that Chris Rock would tell you to cool it.

Their earthly reward for all this effort? The two pizzas and case of cheap beer you order to feed all fifteen volunteers.

Know this: Anyone who helps you move once is a casual idiot. Anyone who helps you twice in this lifetime is still an idiot, but he is the truest friend you will ever have. Improve your karma chain by ordering them a real meal the second time. (No, McDonalds doesn't count.)

So, you ask, how do I embark on this "great American adventure"?

Moving sales are a great way to get rid of your old furniture and help you find a whole new batch of junk to clutter your apartment. You don't really want to dump your $400 Jennifer Convertibles sofabed for $35, do you? No, of course not, but I guarantee you'll find one just like it at a moving sale in your new hometown, all the while sparing you the hassles of heavy lifting with U-Haul. After all, the key to moving successfully lies in being inventive.

Speaking of U-Haul, it's time to give them a call. U-Haul is the way anyone short of the financial status of Michael Jordan moves, and besides, what's the point in hiring a full crew when you'll likely be making that adventurous move all the way across town?

Next you have to actually find a U-Haul truck that's big enough to carry all your junk. While every major city has ample U-Haul dealers, most only have trucks available for those people who are anal-retentive enough to reserve a vehicle six months in advance: In other words, your parents will beat you to a reservation every time.

You, on the other hand, will wake up at 7 A.M. on moving day making more frantic phone calls than a crackhead looking to score some rock, and you'll likely find that the only available truck is at the nearest airport location—meaning nearest to the airport, but six hours' worth of traffic from your current place.

Once you actually get to U-Haul, trust us: Buy boxes from them. You may think you've won some great economic victory if you beg grocery stores for free boxes, but they're likely to be laden with roach eggs and fruit flies. Buy fresh boxes—they're only about a buck apiece. However, if you're still so cheap that even this purchase has to be rationalized, you can always store them for the next move or sell them at the moving-in sale that's so certain to endear you to the neighbors.

ROOMMATES
(OR: THE SIBLINGS YOU NEVER WANTED)

You'll have to be doubly creative in finding a roommate you can both trust and tolerate.

Having a roommate when you're over the age of twenty-five is a sure sign of being a loser. Therefore, you should try to convince all visitors that yours is actually employed as your butler.

However, the harsh light of economic reality often requires you to live with at least one complete stranger when you make your move into the real world. Short of a criminal background check, there's no way of knowing whether this person is a psychopath.

There are several options for finding a roommate:

1. Live with a friend.

This may seem like the easiest and most obvious solution. After all, you've shared many good times with this person, and have occasionally helped each other with your emotional problems. However, this could also be the most dangerous option of all.

If you live with a friend, chances are excellent you will not stay friends for long. After all, you will finally discover your friends' innermost secrets: their personal hygiene, sleep habits, promiscuity levels, and complete lack of musical taste.

Remember that time-honored grammar-school rhyme: Make new friends, keep the old; one is silver, one is gold. If you truly value your friends, then don't drive them away just to save a couple hundred bucks a month.

2. Peruse the newspaper ads.

Ah, the thrill of the unknown! This may sound exotic if you are on a vacation to Borneo or the Amazon rain forest, but it does not apply when meeting people to live with.

They should have a decoder box for roommate ads in the paper. If you see the phrase "cool, laid-back guy," it really means "gay heroin addict." And if it's combined with the phrase "not home much," it means he's on the run from the law right now.

During one search for a roommate in the category of a twentysomething straight white male, Carl answered ads from a thirty-year-old lesbian lawyer, a fifty-five-year-old alcoholic who looked and talked like Dan Aykroyd, and a twenty-nine-year-old black radical who was constantly battling having his phone disconnected. In other words, ads can be incredibly vague.

Like most people, you probably snicker at the thought of meeting your life's romantic match in the love ads. Yet even if you occasionally answer one of those ads (like the people who laugh the hardest at them), the odds of making it through a first date once you both see how much you lied to flatter yourselves are extremely slim. Think of your roommate search as an attempt to find a life partner for a year at a time, and you'll realize just how wrong a newspaper search can be.

3. Hire a placement service.

Anyone who endured the college potluck-roommate system knows just how dangerous this lottery can be. You should have known that leaving your roommate selection up to the whims of the wisecracking interns in the housing office would be a disaster.

In fact, Carl personally spent his first semester away from home living with a walleyed science fiction fan named Matt, who spent his mornings watching *Love Boat* reruns and his evenings enjoying the cult classic series *Beauty and the Beast.* As a bonus, this fine specimen of humanity believed in personally testing the abilities of his superhero creations, spending many a night running through the dormitory hallways while wearing a blindfold, in order to see whether a blind flying superhero was feasible. Matt learned the hard way that the blind have no business flying or running pell-mell through any building when he proceeded to break his arm after tumbling down a flight of concrete stairs.

Finding a good roommate-match service as an adult can be even trickier. You may think that paying the typical $55 fee might help protect you from criminals and flakes, but then again, what criminal or flake can't come up with $55?

The whole idea of a service is kinda weird and creepy anyway. When Carl boldly and foolishly chose to use one, he was met by a woman whose voice was raspier than *Night Court*'s Selma Diamond and faced with a barrage of questions: "Are you willing to live with dogs? Cats? Blacks? Gay guys?"

How do you answer that? If you say no, you're an honorary member of the Klan. If you say yes, you might end up living with a gay cat.

In other words, go back and use your friends after all. Let's face it—that "make new friends, keep the old" crap is straight out of grammar school. In the real world, you lose all your old friends when you or they get married anyway. If you can dupe 'em into sharing a living space with you, drive them away on your terms—one long, grueling year's lease at a time.

Tips for living with roommates:

1) Always keep in mind that killing him/her will only up your share of the rent.

2) Keep bedroom and bathroom doors securely locked. Remember this simple formula: Unwanted Nudity = Expensive Therapy.

3) Keep hope alive—just because your roommate actually has friends and lovers doesn't mean you never will.

4) In college, a dead roommate gets you straight A's; in real life, it gets you indicted.

HOME DECORATION (OR: HOW TO FURNISH YOUR APARTMENT FOR $19.95 OR LESS)

Deciding on appropriate home decor is tough, and having roommates only makes it worse. After all, you already have limited financial resources and bad taste of your own. Now compound that with the problems of an additional roommate or two or three. We think you're starting to get the picture: It's like a furniture showroom without real furniture.

First off, a warning: Never allow anything that is accompanied by a thirty-day free trial period to enter your house. Yes, it sounds tempting to own the Little Rascals commemorative plate sets from the Franklin Mint, to proudly display all of the books in the Time-Life Tales of the Unknown collection upon your bookcase, and to enjoy watching repeat episodes of *Sanford and Son* in Spanish.

But don't do it. These things are embarrassing, immature, and worst of all—actually cost money.

So what to do? Well, my friends, home decorating is where you actually *can* have a great American adventure. There are many ways of scavenging for your possessions, but two particularly favorite games come to our minds:

1. Dumpster Diving.

Yes, you read right. We're advocating your willingness to put aside all thought of personal safety and hygiene in the name of searching for really cool stuff.

Most people are too lazy or embarrassed to spend an afternoon rooting through others' garbage, but if you do find yourself with a spare couple of hours, it can be a lot of fun. You grew up watching Indiana Jones dodge snakes; now in your own, unexotic urban neighborhood, you can dodge rats.

And while you may be forced to outmaneuver the street-wizened competition wrought by full-time dumpster divers, please be courteous to your fellow street urchins and be sure to ask if anyone's sleeping inside before you jump in and claim your territorial rewards.

2. Rolling Thunder.

All this game requires is a pickup truck or a flatbed trailer, a (very) sturdy rope, and a bottle of tequila or other hard liquor. Oh yes, and a friend to drive the truck.

The rope goes around your waist and ties you into the bed of the truck; the tequila is to provide you with the sense of daring that only liquid courage can provide. The friend ties you into the truck bed, hops in the cab, and tears the vehicle through an assortment of your hometown's alleys as you lean off the bed of the truck and grab mattresses, chairs, and other assorted, large, abandoned furniture at speeds of up to sixty-five miles per hour.

Sure, you could just walk up and drag off a mattress like a normal human being, but if there's one thing you learned from us in this book, it's why be normal?

CHAPTER NINE

HOW TO EAT BETTER THAN YOUR PETS

First and foremost, I would like to point out to the reader that the following chapter will not be a lesson in dining etiquette. While the chapter title may seem to be a kooky piece of hilarity on the part of the authors, the simple fact is that most people today consume their food in a fashion so disgusting to watch it is a wonder we all don't eat with blinders on.

Look around next time you take more than three minutes to eat. What do you see? I'll tell you what I see: I see people jamming fat-laden, grease-squirting goo into their mouths with both hands as if they were about to be taken off for a lethal injection. I see men in suits slurping soup without using a spoon. I see highly educated professionals eating caesar salads with their fingers. I see yuppie parents letting their cola-crazed offspring run around screaming in five-star restaurants, smiling with pride as their little darlings parade their snot-spewing nostrils from table to table.

And hey, those are just my relatives . . .

I only wish some of you had one-tenth the table manners of your pets. It would be a major improvement, believe me. At least your dog doesn't lick himself until after he's done eating.

Table manners are dead. Buried. Pushing up daisies.

So what are we to do, knowing that our table manners are nonexistent at best and loathsome at worst? Well, discontinuing eating entirely is not an option since it's a well-known fact that eating helps keep a person from suffering a premature death from terminal skinniness. So by all means as you travel the Highway of Life (or perhaps in your case the Frontage Road of Life) remember to eat every once in a while, even though we have thoroughly established that you are a disgusting, classless, bovine lout when you perform the act of ingestion.

The Center for Disease Control says that by the year 2005 over 80 percent of all Americans will be overweight. They also know that 1 percent of all Americans are likely to be 80 percent overweight. It's also a well-known fact that the 20 percent of the population that will not be overweight in the year 2005 will not be hard to find.

They will all be cast members on *Ally McBeal.*

So how does a person go about feeding himself in the adult world? Most of us learned everything we know about feeding ourselves from our parents. So let us flash back to your day of graduation.

It was their proudest moment, seeing you walk across that stage and accept your diploma from college, and as your mom and dad watched, tears probably trickled down their faces as they realized that they no longer had to pay for every waking need in your life. "Even with that useless art history degree, our baby at least knows how to feed himself," they thought.

How wrong they were. You've been eating ramen noodles for four years now, and they expect you not to starve on your own? You've been consuming a steady diet of frozen pizza, Lite beer, Doritos, Skittles, Wing Dings, and aerosol cheese, and they think you know how to eat without being killed by the substance on your plate?

The fools!

It's a good thing you know exactly what time every night they serve dinner over there at Mom's place, because you are going to be "just dropping in" at that precise time an awful lot in the next several years.

Go ahead and do it. Don't feel guilty. They did it to your grandparents. Can't change the course of evolution.

But eventually, either a desire for self-sufficiency or a restraining order will necessitate you learning how to eat at home. So here's how to do it.

First, let us deconstruct your present diet. The fact that you can now pick up a Whopper at the Shell station is not your salvation when it comes to nutrition, my friend. In fact, it should make you a tad suspicious that the petroleum and fast-food industries feel so cozy with each other.

Cheeseburger . . . gasoline . . . how much do their chemical formulas intersect? Food for thought.

Either way, the people who run the station know one thing—you're going to have gas after you leave.

The *Frankensteinian* chemistry of fast food applies to all of those chips you eat as well. Think about it: Do you really think there is any nutritional value in the powder that makes those nachos "Salsariffic?" Fat chance.

The chemistry of foodstuffs bleeds over into alchemy when it comes to that aerosol cheese. Good heavens! Look at how they spell it! "C H E E Z"

Simple rule of living well, my friend: Never, ever eat misspelled food. If man was meant to eat aerosol food then cows would be made of tin.

And since we are being brutally honest about your pathetic eating choices, let us examine the mainstay of the Dork's Daily Diet: ramen noodles.

"But wait!" you say. "Ramen noodles are only ten cents a pack, and they are noodles! Even my mom makes noodles when I drop in unannounced during the dinner hour . . ." That is true. You mom uses noodles. She even uses her noodle—by never consuming ramen noodles.

Why not?

Just look at that price per package. If it's ten cents a bag, is it likely to be good for you? If it's ten cents a bag, do you really think they offer any nutritional value? What do they make it from? Or do they just find it? Your mother should know.

"But millions of people in China eat ramen every day!" you protest. That's right. That's why we fought the Cold War.

Hey, if you want to slowly deplete your body's precious storehouse of nutrients while munching on Mao Tse-tung's favorite snack, be my guest. It is your choice.

Commie.

CHAPTER TEN

HOW TO DRESS

It has been said that "Clothes make the man." And there are few clichés that ring quite as true as we walk the streets of the adult world. Clothes not only make the man, they often make the man's friends laugh out loud behind his back.

In short, you are now out of college, so the ripped jeans and stained T-shirts are no longer the fashion statement they were in your undergrad years.

Back then, your shoddy attire said: "I am an iconoclast. I care not for the rules and values of your society. I follow my own path and go my own way." Now they say: "I am a slob. Do not hire me. I still follow my own path, but when I get sweaty this shirt makes its own gravy."

Not exactly what you want the execs at the Fortune 500 companies to think about you, is it?

Clothing also is often a big deal-breaker when it comes to a person's love life. In fact, only a person as slovenly as you will overlook a crummy wardrobe. "Hey Mr. Big Shot Author, my clothes aren't old . . . they're retro!" the reader may wheeze. Well just remember, while the "retro" look may be all the rage at certain dance clubs, it gets literally old on a day-to-day basis.

(As you may have noticed this book continuously exhorts you to do . . .) Think, Dear Reader!

If your significant other is wearing duds from the 1970s, what other relics of that misbegotten decade haunt his or her mind? Are you sentencing yourself to night after night of Bee Gees music crackling from the speakers of the 8-track tape deck in her GMC Pacer? Are you ready to live by the standards of 1977?

Remember, the minimum wage then was $2.65 an hour. And apparently the person you are dating is still trying to live on that. So cast off all badly attired lovers and burn the contents of your closet!

"But then what will I wear?" again whines the reader. This is where cable television really earns its keep.

Cable television? You bet! You want to know what to put on your body while you consume your ramen noodles? Well pick up that clicker and turn that dial over to the "E" network. Wait for the commercial break and then . . . buy that stuff!

America is the Great Consumer Society. It is both your right and your duty to consume, consume, consume!

Come on. Do your part for Uncle Sam and drive to the mall. When you get there demand everything you have ever seen hawked on television.

It is of ultimate importance that you do not ever purchase clothing that has not been featured in a multibillion-dollar advertising campaign; otherwise you may as well let your mom dress you. You do remember the way Mom used to dress you, don't you? Well, now the advertising executives on Madison Avenue are taking Mom's place.

Thank God! Unlike your mom, Madison Avenue has no interest in making you look like a dork. Or keeping you celibate until marriage. So walk into the store, step right up to that girl with the pierced lip who is folding the sweaters, and demand she make you look like an ad on the "E" Network.

Refuse to even try on a shirt or pants that you haven't seen on the wriggling bottom of a gorgeous nineteen-year-old dancer in a Gap or Old Navy ad. Buy the hype!

However, in order to literally buy the hype, you will need to pay for all of these clothes. Sooo . . . go to your local bank and demand a $5,000 line of credit solely for the purpose of purchasing khaki clothing. If the bank manager refuses, take him hostage until he gives you *his* khakis. He'll do it if you threaten him just right . . .

We have entered a new millennium where "Khaki Is God." So worship it, you heathen!

I would also like to mention here that it is imperative that any sophisticated wardrobe be augmented with accessories galore.

Accessorizing is ultimately what separates us from the lower primates. Think about it. Ever see a chimpanzee with a really cool pair of shades?

Okay, bad example. We've all seen chimps with a really cool pair of shades. But have you ever seen a chimp in a hilarious feather boa?

Oh yeah. We've all seen that too. Come to think of it, them chimps really know how to dress snazzy. Just don't let a chimp buy clothes for you, or at least go to the store with him. Maybe you'll learn something.

After you and the chimp get all the necessary accessories, you'll need to buy shoes and socks. You'll have to take charge here, because chimps never wear shoes—not even in an Elvis movie.

Shoes are not only fashionable, they are a hygienic necessity as they keep the sidewalks of the world from smelling like feet.

There simply is not a thing I can tell a woman about the buying of, shopping for, or general worshipping of shoes. From the moment of conception all most women ever think about in their spare time is shoes. Someday, when the ladies take over, all men will be forced to work in shoe factories and give foot rubs.

However, the great likelihood is that you have less knowledge of shoes than the chimpanzee you are shopping with.

Men fear shoes. At least I do. So I do what all men do. I ask a woman to pick them out for me while I go over to the cookie store in the mall with my friend the chimp.

At this point you may be wondering why you need clothes at all if you are going to be droning away your life in front of a monitor in your living room.

Good point. I hadn't thought of that actually. Feel free to work naked at home. But for the love of all that is decent at least put a towel on your chair.

By the way—you're still going to have to leave the room occasionally, if only to give the pizza guy his money. So you will still need khakis to wear temporarily to the door. You want to look good for the food delivery folks. One of them could easily end up being Mr. or Ms. Right.

Also, you'll need clothes to wear to the bank when you take the manager hostage, as well as clothes for when you go shopping for clothes. Clothes to shop for clothes?

You betcha! As the sign on the door says: "No Shirt, No Shoes, No Service . . ."

It even says that on the doors of stores that sell shirts and shoes, which makes no sense really. Because, if you think about it, a shoeless customer should in fact be a pretty easy sale at a store that handles footwear. But what do I know?

A final word on the subject of how to dress:

You may have noticed that this chapter does not actually deal with the mechanics of putting on your clothes.

Again there is an old saying that is pertinent here: "Everyone puts their pants on one leg at a time." The saying is supposed to tell us that we are all equal. It is a stupid saying. I say go ahead and jump into those khakis, feet first and simultaneously.

Do it for Old Glory.

And Old Navy.

CHAPTER ELEVEN

~~~~~

MANNERS, AND HOW TO FOOL FOLKS INTO THINKING YOU HAVE THEM

The modern man and woman do not, it would seem, place a great deal of value on what used to be termed "manners." Whether this is a good thing or not is truly a matter of interpretation by the reader, as societal norms have been in constant flux over the past three decades, and we live in a world that cherishes the rights of the individual above all else.

Okay. Read the last paragraph again. Do you have any idea what it means? Of course not!

Really, all the paragraph contained was a vague bundle of excuses for the lack of kindness and consideration that most everyone, myself included, displays toward everyone else these days.

Boy, have we become a bunch of clods!

We have become a society that can use gibberish at will merely so *we can avoid manners!* I mean, for Pete's sake . . . "societal norms?" The phrase makes no sense to me and I'm the one who typed it.

But when I sit on the subway, with my briefcase occupying the seat adjacent, I need not worry that my comfort inconveniences anyone else. Even as a pregnant mother of two stands one foot in front of me, I can use clever verbal excuses to ease my conscience as I ignore her and keep sitting . . .

See—I am not an egocentric blob of protoplasm without even a scintilla of decency or breeding. Oh no. I am merely a Postmodern American Male.

Those wild and wacky societal norms!

Phrases like "societal norms" are merely a nice way of saying that the world has become a beehive full of selfish louts literally stepping on each other's toes without so much as an "Oops! That looked painful, dude!" in apology.

Think about it.

When was the last time you called an older woman "Ma'am"? When was the last time you started an order in a restaurant with "Please" and ended it with "Thank you"? When was the last time you said the phrase "Have a nice day" and didn't mean exactly the opposite? Been a while hasn't it?

Me too!

What in the name of societal norms has happened to us?

While our parents may have almost annihilated the population of the planet with two World Wars and a Cold War, at least they held the bloody door for each other!

Be honest, Dear Reader. You couldn't care less if the entire outside world perished in a hurricane of flaming sulfur, as long as it didn't interrupt whatever *you* were doing at the moment. *Hey . . . whatever . . . as long as the sulfurous flames don't knock out the satellite dish.* How sad.

Manners, more than our ability to manipulate stock markets or excel at video games, are really the basis of a decent society. At least that's what the elderly disabled man standing on the bus said to me as I sat in the designated handicapped seat.

And ignored him.

So as a service to the young men and women reading this book, may I give you all a brief primer on basic societal decency.

You may feel free to tell me to "talk to the hand" as I blather on. In fact, feel free to ignore me. I'll just stand here and talk. Blah blah blah . . .

First and foremost, manners are based on a concept that has been entirely banished from society by MTV, convenience stores, and the entire "in your face" Internet society.

Believe it or not, you are not The Center of the Entire Universe!!!

Okay, take a breath. I know that last sentence probably scared you. I mean, it goes against everything you have ever seen demonstrated by the people who shaped your morality as a youth.

Of course, I'm not referring to your parents, teachers, clergy, and civic leaders. What could they possibly have had to do with shaping your morals and ethics?

I am, of course, referring to the real guardians of the postmodern era: MTV, convenience stores, and the entire "in your face" Internet society.

So, let me say it again, new Adult-A-Reenos! All of the cosmos does not revolve around you and your needs. The Hubble Space Telescope even has the photos to prove it.

We have become convinced that we are entitled to twenty-four–hour attention and entertainment, twenty-four–hour access to our money, food, sexual desires, and overall pleasure. Well, guess what? We aren't!

Okay, take another breath. I know I'm moving fast here.

So, do you want to know where the avalanche of horrible manners really begins? Well, I'm going to tell you anyway.

All bad manners begin in the same place: at the store where you bought that cellular phone you carry around all the time.

Remember the day you got that demonic conduit of ruthless and rude telecommunication? Sure you do!

You walked into the cellular phone store, forgot to hold the door for the nun behind you, and cut ahead in line. Then you demanded, without using the words "please" or "thank you," that you be hooked up with a phone *immediately!* And the boob behind the counter took your order and filled it without even protesting your abusive behavior. Because, by God, you needed that phone right away! I mean, what if you were to miss a call? Somebody could be trying to reach you! Right now!

So what if the ringing of the headpiece interrupts the wedding of your best friend? The wedding can wait. There are always weddings. This call . . .

Could be important.

Admittedly, it would be the first time ever that an important call was received by the owner of a cell phone.

But who knows? You've got to answer that ringing little receiver of Hades!

Listen up, people of Earth! That call can wait! How do I know for sure? Because I too own a cell phone and I have never, ever, gotten a call on it that was necessary.

Nobody I know ever has gotten a truly necessary, "let's interrupt the baptism" phone call. Nobody you know has, and believe me—*you* haven't.

So you want to start a Renaissance of Manners? You want to bring decency back to the public discourse? You want to feel the illusion of safety in your car again?

Well, the answer is not blowing in the wind,

my friend. Nope. The answer is ringing in your pocket.

So turn off your stupid cell phone in the movie theatre! Turn off your stupid cell phone in the restaurant! Turn off your stupid cell phone on the bus! In the funeral parlor! The birthing room! The jury box!

TURN OFF YOUR STUPID CELL PHONE . . . PERIOD!

Another thing about your phone deserves mentioning. I'll bet it doesn't just ring, does it?

Oh no! Heaven forbid! How boring!

You deserve to be entertained, even by the phone you don't really need as you take that incredibly unimportant incoming call.

No, your phone probably plays a bit of Beethoven's Fifth Symphony when someone calls you, doesn't it? Just enough of Beethoven's Fifth to amuse you . . . and annoy everyone else in the movie theatre.

It's times like these when I'm sure that Beethoven himself is glad he is both deaf and dead.

So, you want to do your part for good manners? It's simple.

Go to a hardware store . . . buy a hammer . . . take out your cell phone . . . and smash it.

Who knows? Maybe you'll start a trend. Maybe the rest of the world, inspired by your brave sacrifice of this ubiquitous electronic nuisance, will go to a hardware store and smash *their* phones. Maybe, just maybe, while all of this demolition is going on, somebody will inadvertently hold the door for someone else.

Or say "please."

Or wait their turn in line.

Patiently, and with dignity.

Maybe, just maybe, a tidal wave of decency and courtesy will sweep the land. All because you had the foresight and vision to annihilate your phone and acknowledge the rest of us.

Politely.

It is a dream I have.

CHAPTER TWELVE

So You Want a Committed Relationship

Now that the ivy-covered halls of either your school or the asylum are behind you, and you are setting off into the terrifying territory of adulthood, chances are you want that special something that troubadours throughout history have called True Love.

Well, good luck, buckaroo. Now you've really asked for it.

Relationships are tricky, even dangerous, and it's not bad advice to tell the reader that a life of celibate solitude has its charms. It is also good advice to tell you that you should never ingest alcohol, but since you very well might have been boozed up when you decided to buy this book, there's a fat chance you'll hear that from me.

You may already consider yourself to be in a committed relationship. "Hey!" you might say, "There's a woman who calls me every day to ask about my life!"

That woman is a collection agent. She's not in love. She's working on commission. Sorry to burst that particular bubble.

No, no, no, Dear Reader, the committed person you seek as a permanent (or at least pleasantly temporary) life partner is not going to call you at home spontaneously and with no previous visual contact. Which is too bad, because otherwise your dubious finances and underdeveloped sense of hygiene might just be considered wonderful personality traits.

But they aren't. You are the slob you believe
yourself to be. Fixing that is another chapter
entirely. Right now we're talking about finding a
mate for the present version of you, imperfect as
that may be . . . And it is.

So where does a person find a friend (well, not
a friend exactly, because frankly most of your
friends have no interest in what you are planning to
do with the "friend" we are talking about locating)
in such a big and impersonal world?

No secret there, really. No matter where you
live, city or country, suburb or small town, the
source for lifelong romance is right there, in your
neighborhood. It has been there all along waiting
for you to come back to it, to reembrace it and its
wonderful customs, ceremonies, and traditions.
The place where you will find true and meaningful
love, lifelong love, is under your very nose, and the
wonderful community of people who meet there
every week want you to join in their celebration.

So get out of your chair and go there!

I am talking about your local sports bar. They are waiting. They even have some special drinks that accelerate the falling-in-true-love process.

Most everyone meets his life partner in a bar. It is where I met my life partner. It is where you'll meet yours.

I can hear some of you complaining about that last statement. "But I don't want to meet my lifelong love at a place that serves Jalapeño Poppers!" you are saying.

Okay. Fine. Do it the hard way.

You snob.

Reject my thoroughly researched advice and data.

I do and do and do for you people and this is the thanks I get . . .

So here are some ways to meet people to love away from the bar you'll eventually end up at anyway:

1. Church Groups.

Lots of fun here . . . Whether it's a quilting bee or the Annual Abstinence Jamboree, nothing beats the celibate clergy for setting up a romantic mood for others. There will be plenty of punch, cookies, and popcorn, as well as a safe, sensible, and sane atmosphere for meeting people.

Just one question: Do you really want to fall in love in a safe, sensible, and sane atmosphere?

Probably not. In fact I don't advise it. But it's up to you.

At least when it is all over you'll have a quilt . . .

2. Personal Ads.

Yeah right. That'll make for a lovely story to tell the grandkids.

"That's right honey, Grandma and I never would have met if it weren't for that ad in *The Penny-Saver.*"

Now that's romantic, and if you're really lucky, you'll not only meet the person of your dreams, you'll get a great deal on a used lawn mower. All in the same day. All for just the fifty-cent price of a newspaper.

"Okay wise guy, what's wrong with that?" you may well ask.

Let's just say I don't believe in looking for love at the bottom of a birdcage.

3. Blind Dates.

Good Lord, have you sunk that low? Can't you even afford to buy an ad in *The Penny-Saver*?

All right then, fine. Go on that blind date your drinking buddy set up for you.

But ask yourself one thing. If this person you are meeting sight unseen is so great, then why didn't your friend ask him/her/it out?

Huh?

Huh?

You know damn well why. Let the buyer beware . . . Just consider the adjective "blind." Is it usually a word we associate with good things? Not unless you're blind drunk it isn't.

HOLD ON THERE, BUDDY!
(Or: One Place You Should
Never Look for a Date.)

So you think you're ready to begin the arduous process known as Adult World Dating. Ah yes, this is the time of your life when the possibilities seem endless, yet only rarely present themselves if you are genetically incapable of looking like Brad Pitt or Julia Roberts.

We've already covered some of the most likely venues to score a date or mate, but one thing we want to clearly impress upon you is: The Importance of Avoiding Action in the Workplace.

Forget all the problems that stem from the inevitable sexual harassment lawsuit any female coworker will level against you for asking her out. Dating inside the workplace is just plain embarrassing and impractical.

Of course, it's bad enough if the date goes poorly and you have to awkwardly encounter the other person at the copy machine on a daily basis. Not to mention the sheer ugliness involved in passing stories back and forth about each other to everyone else in the building. Trust us: One bad date within your office, no matter how large the corporation, and you will never be able to enter the office dating pool again.

If the date goes well, you're soon either fervently hiding your coupled status due to your company's anti-dating policies, or you're going to become the incessant object of watercooler conversation. Frankly, based on our years of corporate workplace experience, both will happen.

This means you will have to share your happiness *and* your unpleasant relationship moments (and trust us, they will occur) with not only each other, your families, friends, and your nosy neighbors, but also with every boss and coworker who notices you're still wearing the same clothes you had on the night before but were too lazy to change when you slept over at your beloved's.

Everyone will stare with either disgust or leering curiosity each time you shoot each other a coy glance after a night of blissful passion or a look of abject disdain after your ten-thousandth fight about the proper place for clipping your toenails. They will snicker cruelly as they place and collect money in the weekly betting pool that focuses solely on the prospects for your long-term happiness.

And if either of you is in a position of authority over the other, good luck ever gaining any respect for your relationship, even if you wind up married to each other. Sure, you can reap the ample rewards of receiving presents from hundreds of butt-kissing underlings, but remember one thing: Whoever has the lesser job will always be seen as having slept their way to the top—or at least to middle management.

So that's it. That's all I can say about finding that someone special.

Get thee to a sports bar!

CHAPTER THIRTEEN

ADVICE TO THE MEN ABOUT YOUR "SENSE OF STYLE" (OR: HOW ARE YOU EVER GONNA GET LUCKY LOOKING LIKE THAT?)

You've heard it all your life, from your mom, your teachers, your grandma, and every old lady who ever decided to stick her nose into your existence: "Are you actually going out dressed like that?"

Sad to say, you should really pay attention to them; after all, they are women.

You may have forgotten this because of your complete lack of desire to sleep with them, but nonetheless they share the same strange set of standards as all the women you so fervently hope to meet someday. They expect you to keep your pants pressed, your shoes polished, and your shirt unstained. In other words, they expect the impossible.

We are merely suggesting you listen to what their complaints are so that you may devise ways to counteract and subvert them.

The greatest way to overcome female criticism is by establishing a sense of confidence and charm. A great man knows how to discuss many topics, so watch lots of television and describe it as "research." After all, nothing intrigues a woman more than the conversational fodder you gleaned about Hitler on the History Channel, or the mating rituals of the praying mantis you watched on Discovery.

Secondly, lose every T-shirt and tattoo you ever owned. Their slogans and imagery contain nothing of significance or attraction for a woman, and even your guy friends don't really think the Budweiser slogan on a T-shirt is funny once you hit the age of thirty.

They also create a sense of downright shame when you consider the fact that our Founding Fathers fought and died for your hard-won American right to wear the "Spam" logo on your chest. And besides, don't you realize that *you're* going to hate yourself when you turn sixty-five and see the Def Leppard logo still tattooed on your sagging pecs?

Basically, we're throwing in the towel on the style question. Women have made it too damned complicated to try to fight them on this one. Instead of trying to stand out from the crowd, you should be trying to look like the guys in all those clothing commercials and L. L. Bean catalogs. Sure, they're not even attracted to women in real life, but their unceasing ability to maintain a crease in their Gap khakis and keep their CK underwear truly tighty and whitey gives women hope that somewhere out there is a man who knows how to keep his shirts as straight as his sexuality. Spend a couple bucks at the local cleaners each week and you'll give her the illusion that *you are that man.*

CHAPTER FOURTEEN

TWO PATHETIC MEN'S ADVICE ON DATING ETIQUETTE

First, a disclaimer: Tim's romantic instincts were put into mothballs twenty years ago because he's only had to impress the woman who is his wife, and Carl has been in even worse shape: He can go from windswept start to dramatic finish in three quick dates. He consoles himself with the thought that while ladies may find him to be a waste of their time, he still has them lining up because they can experience the entire arc of a relationship while only losing a month of their dating lives.

So you've mustered the courage to ask that special someone out. It's only natural that you'd have some questions. And—you guessed it—we're here to offer our solutions!

1. Wining and dining.

When you were in college, wining and dining seemed to consist solely of tapping a keg and consuming as much alcohol as possible, while eating foods exclusively from the basic pepperoni and sausage food group. But now that you've earned your degree and have landed a job that can afford tastes more expensive than a Little Caesar's Two-for-One special, the choices become more complex.

Wining a woman as a fully functioning adult means not only buying wine, *but actually offering her some of it.* "But that's expensive!" you blurt. Yes, it can be, but remember you're after that most priceless of objects—the human heart—and she knows you were dumb enough to sign up for a Mastercard your senior year. Just order her a glass. Or two.

If you're concerned that your lack of French fluency skills might make you look stupid, fine: Let her order the wine for herself and face the humiliation of the Bilingual Challenge. Better yet, tell the waiter to bring you a glass of the most expensive wine he or she has to offer, and instead of worrying about what château it came from, reduce the choices to categories you could have understood in kindergarten: Red or White.

As far as dining goes, these simple tips should help in navigating the waters:

- You can tell it's a fancy restaurant if the chef's name is on the door, there's no ketchup on the table, and the menu is more than one page and isn't covered in plastic.

- You can tell it's not fine dining when the menu consists of an overhead, electrically lit board with a Coca-Cola logo emblazoned across it. It is also not fine dining if it includes the word "fries" or "combo" anywhere on the menu.

- Never order the chef's omelette surprise without actually meeting the chef. Before you get surprised with anything in an eating situation, you'll want to be able to recognize his face in a police lineup.

2. Other social occasions.

Of course, your date won't start *and* end with the meal. That is, unless you're *really* unlucky; Carl once spent ninety minutes on a date, from pickup to drop-off, and each one of those minutes was more excruciating than the last.

No, the traditional American date moves on from dinner to either a movie or dancing. (Don't worry, guys—we'll get to the sex!)

Rule No. 1 about dancing: There is nothing less sexy than a white guy learning how to mambo. Avoid foreign dance clubs at all costs.

Rule No. 2 about dancing: There is nothing less sexy than *any* guy attempting *any* dance. Just don't do it.

On the other hand, the moviegoing experience is a time-honored American tradition. Hell, we invented the movies! And with more than four hundred films being made and released into theaters each year, there are plenty of choices to be had. You can drag her into a pistol-packing action movie, or take the smart route and let her lure you into a tear duct activating chick-fest romance picture.

Just remember one thing:

- Never let a woman on a first date see that your idea of a great date is a video double feature of *Taxi Driver* and *Midnight Cowboy,* followed by making out to "Let's Pretend We're Married" by Prince. Save that for the *fourth* date, to mix things up a little just when she thinks she's getting to know you.

After all, there's nothing more important than preserving that sense of intrigue. However, this principle doesn't go both ways:

- Always learn as much as possible about a woman before asking her out—or you could find yourself dating a feng shui consultant who talks to lightpoles. (Again, this happened to Carl.)

After all, the most terrifying statement in the English language is, "There's a lot you don't know about me," accompanied by a throaty, maniacal laugh.

But who are we kidding? There are certain times of the year when you will go out with *anybody*. The holidays are the worst for that. You don't care if they're missing a leg, some teeth, or their left eyeball—you need someone to kiss at midnight on New Year's Eve.

SEXUAL SITUATIONS
(OR: THE REALLY GOOD PARTS YOU
WAIT FOR IN CABLE MOVIES BUT RARELY
EXPERIENCE IN YOUR EVERYDAY LIFE)

See, we told you we'd get to sex! (Even if Carl rarely
if ever has, and Tim has long since surrendered to
the barren wasteland known as marriage.)

Because we so rarely get to actually partake of
sex, a few simple rules will have to suffice.

- Never confuse sex with love. You can lead
  a very fulfilling life without love.

- By the third date, you need to consult a
  phone chart: Should you call her every
  day, or every two days?

- When attending an orgy, always bring a
  magazine in case you're just not included.

- For heaven's sake, don't worry if you're
  shy in a group-sex situation. At a swingers

party, conversation is usually not an issue. What are you going to discuss anyway—the geopolitical climate of Central America?

- To ensure you show all women proper respect, treat them as if they were your little sister. (This rule does not apply south of the Mason–Dixon line.)

- If you want to know what she'll look like when she's old, look at her mom. If you want to know what she'll be like in bed when she is old, sleep with her mom.

SECTION THREE

SEIZE THE TOILET PAPER

At this point, Dear Reader, you must notice that the book doesn't have many more pages left. There is a good reason for this. You are nearing the end of it. And by "it" we not only mean the book, but we also mean the end of what we have to tell you. It is time for you to move on, Dear Reader; time not only to face the music, but perhaps even turn the music down a little so other people in the apartment can get some sleep. It is time for you to read the last couple of chapters, get off the pot, and get on with your so-called existence.

So enjoy these last pages, and don't forget to buy whatever book we write as a follow-up to this one.

CHAPTER FIFTEEN

HOW TO COPE WITH YOUR PREDICTABLE LACK OF SUCCESS

The great Vince Lombardi once said: "Winning isn't everything, it's the only thing." I'm sure he believed this was true when his Green Bay Packers won the first two Super Bowls, but a little while later when he died it would seem that he found out the hard way that there are things other than winning. Especially when playing games with the Grim Reaper.

As Americans we are obsessed with winning, largely because we've never had Visigoths or Vikings or any other army beginning with the letter "V" march into our country and take it over. Another big factor in our denial of both Death and its pesky baby brother, Defeat, is the imagery we have all been bombarded by in television commercials.

Think about all of those commercials. All those happy people. Winners all.

Think of the constant imagery bombarding your cranium of average guys finding out that the key to having sex with supermodels is simply having the foresight and presence of mind to purchase and drink the right "Lite beer."

But what do those models really drink?

It ain't Lite beer, Einstein. It's bottled water.

And who buys the bottled water for the super-models? Not average guys . . .

Defeat is all around. It is as ubiquitous as sewer water and it stinks twice as bad. Every single day something defeats us in some small way, whether it is the parking ticket on our windshield, the tele-marketer who interrupts us while we are trying to watch porno, or the rabid squirrel that takes an interest in us when we go for a relaxing walk in the park.

So what can we do in the face of all of this disappointment?

Well, first let us deconstruct Vince Lombardi's preposterous slogan. If old Vinnie could come back from the Great Beyond, he'd admit that he was wrong about winning being the only thing.

But he can't. He's dead. The loser.

So learn this new and improved version of the saying. This next sentence will make things a great deal easier as you travel down the Highway of Life:

"Winning isn't everything; it is the least likely thing."

Just look at the odds, Dear Reader . . . There are six billion people living on the planet right now. Six billion working, sweating, striving, and, most likely, losing people.

That's a lot of people. A lot of second-place finishes. Hell, forget second place. You could finish in billionth place in your competition and still be ahead of five billion other shmoes . . .

We're Number One Billion and One! Yahoo.

So obviously, learning to accept your complete mediocrity could very easily be the key to your ultimate success in life. So how do we get in touch with our Inner Loser and find true happiness? Here are a few tried and true methods:

1. Blame your lack of success on others.

This one never fails. In fact it is the only unfailing thing a failure can really rely on.

Think about it. When it comes right down to it the whole world really *is* against you, from the guy who cuts you off on the expressway to the massive goon who takes your wallet in the alley. You aren't paranoid at all when you suspect that people are saying unflattering things behind your back.

They are. There is an endless laughtrack in this world, and all of the jokes are at your expense. Ha Ha Ha . . . So stand up, and let the truth be known.

Everything that has gone or will go wrong in your life is somebody else's fault!

Remember: It isn't whether you win or lose, it's how you lay the blame.

2. Remember that defeat has its advantages.

This is a subtle, rather Zen Buddhist concept, but once you master it you are in like Flynn (whoever Flynn was and wherever he was in . . .).

Think of it this way. Somebody has unfairly, either through a better font on their résumé or with help from a relative in the firm, taken your dream job from you before you even got to the interview. Forget the fact you overslept or showed up with a piece of toilet paper stuck to your shoe; somebody took your gig!

Well, good for him, the ratbastard!

Let him live with the guilt of hurting you. Let him live with the long hours. Let him live with the happy family and humongous house. Let him have it all!

You've got your freedom! You've got your dignity! (At least by your definition . . .) And most important: You've got excuses galore! And no one, no matter how big or small they are, can take that away from you.

You didn't want that stupid dream job anyway. You are just fine right where you are. Living freely on your own time. Coming and going as you please. Even if you are enjoying all of this freedom while living in a soggy refrigerator box in an alley.

3. Put on a happy face!

This is the final and really most effective way to deal with failure and disappointment. Already, I can hear the reader objecting . . . "'Put on a Happy Face'? What kind of Pollyanna hogwash is that?"

Well, Dear Reader, it ain't the kind of hogwash you are thinking at all. These days a happy face comes in the form of what political analysts call "Spin."

And what is spin? That's simple. "Spin" is simply couching everything that happens to you in pleasant terms. Pleasant, untruthful terms.

So spin away! You aren't a desolate loser with no friends . . . You are a Loner in Search of Inner Meaning.

Oooohhhh . . . That sounds deep.

You aren't a pinhead who still lives in his parents' basement . . . You are Exploring Your Ancestral Heritage While Trailblazing the New Extended Family.

You aren't about to meet your demise in an airline disaster . . . You are Taking Advantage of the New Gravity-Assisted Early Landing Program.

You get the idea.

You are doing just fine. Most of us aren't winning—or even aware that we are in the game at all, really. We're all kind of fibbing about how well it is going. We're all fibbing to ourselves that we will live forever. We're all in on the Big Secret . . .

So wear your defeat and failure with pride. Just don't show that pride to anybody else.

And remember, winning isn't everything.

So you damn well better enjoy the victory when you do.

CHAPTER SIXTEEN

IN WHICH ALL THE
LOOSE ENDS TIE UP NEATLY

By now, Dear Reader, you have most likely noticed that the title of this book is *Life: The Final
Frontier* . . . If you haven't, then chances are you
cannot read this chapter at all, and should be in
another part of the bookstore looking at something
with pop-up pictures in it.

We chose the title as a reference to living, as the
Buddhists say, "in the now."

We hope that we have been helpful. No, no, not
just helpful, dammit! We hope our book has proven

positively invaluable in guiding our readers into happy and successful lives, careers, and relationships.

But we sincerely doubt it.

I mean . . . duh! It's just a book. And even worse—it's one of those books you find in the "Humor" section. Invaluable guides to happy lives are over in the "Self-help" section. And don't get your hopes up about "Self-help" either. You may not be helpable. Even by others, so what makes you think you can ever hope to help yourself?

Now that's food for thought in an intellectually anorexic world.

Frankly, since most of us believe in life after death, then life is not the "final frontier." If you believe in the afterlife then at best this life is the penultimate frontier.

Hmmm. *Life: The Penultimate Frontier.* Yeah, right . . . Just try to get a book with a title like *that* to sell more than a dozen copies.

See, while life may be the final frontier, it's life after death that most of us are really banking on. At least I am. Think about it. We get to correct all of the pathetic choices we make in *this* life in the hereafter.

Talk about a cosmic do-over!

Since the great majority of the world believes that a heaven, a hell, and perhaps a purgatory await us all when we shuffle forth from this mortal coil, then why worry about what happens on Earth?

Because maybe . . . this *is* the final frontier.

Now *that* is an unsettling thought. From my point of view, there had better be a life after death, or that psychic I've been sending checks to every month has a lot of explaining to do.

Naaahhh . . . There is an afterlife. Trust us. We haven't lied to you at all during the entire length of this book and we damn sure aren't about to start now!

There is not only a God and an afterlife and a heaven and a hell and a purgatory, there is a reason we are all here. And it isn't only to provide food for the cockroaches when they finally pass humanity on the food chain and ascend the throne as Dominators of the Earth.

I mean, don't get me wrong—the cockroaches *are* going to pass us . . . And we *will* provide them with food.

But that's not the only reason we're here. At least I hope it isn't.

We're here to make the world a better place. Even if it is ultimately only to benefit the enormous insects of the future.

We are here to make Earth the bestest damn Earth it can be! By golly!

Hmmm . . . At first, that whole "by golly" thing seemed to be the perfect ending to our book, but now we suspect you are actually disappointed.

Well . . . Sor-ry!!!!

Have you ever tried to end a book? It's hard!

And you ain't ever tried to do it, that's for sure. So who are you to judge us?

I mean, seriously, did you even read this book in order? Did you start at page one, read the foreword and the introduction and all the pages with small Roman numerals at the bottom instead of real numbers, then proceed to a careful examination of each chapter, in order?

Did you!?

We didn't think so. We knew you wouldn't. So we didn't even write it in order.

That's right. We, the venerable authors of this book that you are currently reading (most likely as you sit upon your toilet), had no plan when we wrote this.

We had no plan . . . and we stuck to it. A couple of guys named Tim and Carl wrote this book, supposedly to give you advice on how to live your life.

And you bought it.

Well, now that you have finished the book, and perhaps even have finished your task on the commode, do you feel we have taught you anything about living?

Of course you don't.

And we most certainly are not sorry. However, the fact that we aren't sorry does not mean we have no fear of being sued by any or all of our readers.

So by the advice of our lawyers, here is some real living advice:

1. Wash your hands before, after, and preferably during every meal.

2. Flush the toilet, you slob.

3. Try only to lie about important things—don't waste your dishonesty on trivial matters!

4. Learn to laugh at yourself, because God knows everybody else is laughing at you.

So good-bye, and thanks for buying our book. That's it.

In Which All the Loose Ends Tie Up Neatly

Well? What the hell are you still reading for?

I just said "Good-bye," for Pete's sake!

The book is over. Put it down. Let someone else into the bathroom for once.

Stop reading! You are done; we are done; the whole experience here is done. So quit bothering us already.

We've held up our end of the bargain. We wrote you a book. Now go live your lives.

And don't call your lawyers either . . . Because according to our lawyers, you have no case. You bought it, you read it, and if you didn't like it you should just wrap it and give it as a gift to someone you aren't too fond of.

Hey! Now that actually *is* good advice!

That's it.

We're out of here.